Dear Acquaintance

Gary Leonard Hammond

Published by Brown Shoes Publishing

garyleonardhammond@gmail.com

Cover design by G. L. Hammond
All Photographs by G. L. Hammond
"Shots from the Loft"

ISBN 978-1-7635521-0-4

Printed and published in Australia

During the winter of 2023, after hitting a creative roadblock, Gary embarked on an eight week writing mission, while living in a rented loft, perched above an old Victorian building in inner city Melbourne.

Gary's loft was a sanctuary, a place where thoughts flowed freely, unburdened by the distractions of the outside world.

The loft's walls absorbed his words, becoming a canvas for his literary brushstrokes.

Eight weeks passed in a blur.

Within these pages lies the results.

For

Marion

and

Georgia

Contents

MY BROWN SHOES

My brown shoes fit me well
but it was a squeeze
I had to quell my instincts
but their approval I believed
was guaranteed
the colour won't offend
and they are the latest trend in modern footwear
many greetings I've received
in my brown shoes

I fixed the buckles fast
that's common sense
they'd last almost a lifetime
the salesman claimed, and corns and bunions
they'd prevent
with matching socks and a tie
you can't deny my fair and rightful place
as part of the establishment
in my brown shoes

They support both arch and heel
a prudent choice
with broad appeal and style
I always walk with ease and pride
and perfect poise
and from those who know what's best
they say I've passed the test without a hitch
there's so much to enjoy
in my brown shoes

FAITH

A light appears, thin but bright
the dark is pierced, from up above
we seize our place, within its blush
we bask and wallow
we claim it for our own
and call it love

The light then dims, and it's dark again
we stumble and limp, like derelict waifs
but then a rumour
filters home
a flash, a glimpse
we claim it as a fact
and call it faith

AFTER

After
the mob have fled
their feigned high spirit's mute
when gathered empires fall, I'll still
be here

After
your current thirst
is quelled and hunger dulls
and desolation jolts, I'll still
be here

And when
your powers cease
and flesh and blood relents
when bygone deeds are shunned, I will
be here

DAMAGED

Damaged, bent and overwhelmed
the past has not been kind
no prototypes to emulate
no fruit upon the vine

Your trust betrayed, your innocence
deceived and drained of life
your future days forever touched
your eyes forever blind

Blind to all you could have seen
to all you could have found
they trampled on the fledging spark
and put the fire out

SECRECY

A quiet moment spent with you, a sanctuary dark and still
they cannot see us hiding here, submerged in secrecy
they cannot see our imperfections
be critical of all we've done
or taunt us with their anecdotes
of dealing with adversity
and how they think we should conduct our lives
advise that's free, but never asked for once
by you or me

We stay concealed and watertight, outside their reach and their
control
they cannot see us if we stay, behind our bolted gate
barely seen we stay protected
from outside weight and influence
nothing stings we're unaffected
if we don't miscalculate
and if we stay within this quiet moment
not tempting fate, the danger that surrounds
will soon abate

But can we stay disguised forever, is it wise or even clever?
to show the world a vacant stare, an uncommitted pose
to leave without a single trace
no parting gift, no rationale
it's surely better to embrace
the aftermath, the highs, the lows
And boldly walk into a thorny patch
and pluck a rose, and welcome all who aid
and who oppose

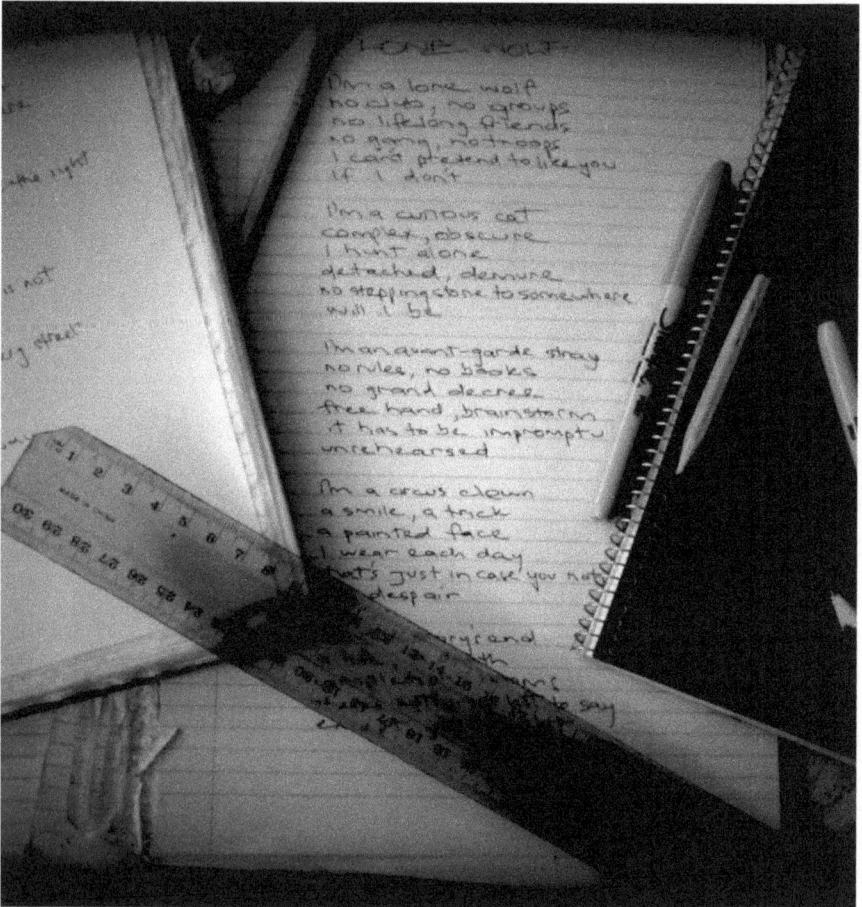

LONE WOLF

I'm a lone wolf
no clubs, no groups
no lifelong friends
no gang, no troop
I can't pretend to like you
if I don't

I'm a curious cat
complex, obscure
I hunt alone
detached, demure
no stepping stone to somewhere
will I be

I'm an avant-garde stray
no rules, no books
no grand decree
free hand, brainstorm
it has to be impromptu
unrehearsed

I'm a circus clown
a smile, a trick
a painted face
I wear each day
what's just in case you no...
...despair

I BUILT A MODEL AEROPLANE.

I built a model aeroplane
and proudly showed it off
it had intricate parts and working pieces
all designed by me
and built by me
it was special like me
and complex like me
it had genius, creativity and flair
like me
I wondered if it was the finest model aeroplane
ever made

I started to look at others to compare
they were better than mine
they were amazing, they were incredible
I couldn't believe how good they were
mine had flaws that now became apparent
it was ordinary like me
it was bland like me
it was a cliche, insipid and common
like me
I hated it
one day I smashed it into a thousand pieces

GREEN AND TENDER

I read you died, still green and tender
suicide, said the press release
no note was left
to clarify
your situation
they said you'd tried so hard
but now you are at peace

I contemplate, your state of mind
did you awake, and wonder when
the pain would stop
advantage shift
and bring relief
was there something else that happened
that pushed you off the edge?

I think I know that deep ravine
way down below, you fell into
I saw it once
while teetering
upon the brink
so I won't stand in judgement
like others seem to do

I TOOK A RANDOM SHOT

I took a random shot I must confess
A wager made; the wheel of fortune spun
That may be how I got into this mess

A desperado's last chance to impress
A single bullet left inside the gun
I took a random shot I must confess

I missed the mark by plenty more or less
I rolled the dice though blinded by the sun
That may be how I got into this mess

Each loss increased my longing for success
I should have stopped before I had begun
I took a random shot I must confess

I should have been a tramp with no address
Instead of seeking love where there was none
That may be how I got into this mess

I should have been a priest then I could bless
Every mother's daughter or their son
I took a random shot instead and yes
That may be how I got into this mess

IN ALL THOSE YEARS

I did not hear you speak
a single word of love
in all those years
not once, not ever
though you were deft
at sneers and jibes
and ridiculing tender spots
to bruise, decry and denigrate

I never saw you give
a whit of heart or grace
in all that time
you saved no room
for thoughtfulness
you'd ride and curse
those tendencies to aid and comfort
to reassert your sovereignty

I never saw you touch
another to declare
devotedness
you scared them off
with a curt demeanour
dressed up and displayed
as a character trait, robust and hardy
but you were afraid, I know that now

FEARLESS HEARTS

We started out with fearless hearts and faith unwavering
doubt had not yet reached our pure intent
and passion was the primal spur that shaped our tunnel vision
that no good sense could throw off-course
defer or disengage
impede or circumvent

Good results in early days would strengthen our resolve
our journey would proceed triumphantly
no qualms we had about our goal, our destiny, our purpose
we brushed aside the cynic's call
and told them "watch and learn"
our rise a certainty

But then a small misstep or two began to blur our picture
faithlessness once born, grew deep and wide
and soon the faintest hint of fear became a fact of life
this judgement made upon ourselves
weighed near a thousand tons
and could not be denied

The vision we once stood by, slowly faded from our view
our boldness and our daring now unnerved
we settled for a place a few miles short of what we'd craved
and wrote it off as fate
though some would say we got
what we deserved

THE WALL

I've heard them talk of life beyond these walls
they say it's wonderful, a paradise
so I sought a harmless route, devoid of danger
but such an odyssey I could not find
And so, I asked a local man for guidance
he smiled and said "I know a trick or three"
he took my coins, but I was unenlightened
still unaware of how I should proceed
I sat and I reflected on my story
the walls still cast a shadow on my days
I grew morose and glum, then quite abruptly
a wise man came to me and did explain
"Proceed as if your goals have all been scored
and you will see, there never was a wall"

EXPOSED

I'll badger, beleaguer, and bother you
and question your beliefs
I'll never do what you think I will
but I'll steer you through the squall and tempest
to a place you've never been

You'll despair and feel uncomfortable
you'll think that I'm contrary
a bucketful of buttonholes
to throw up binds and turning points
before you're good and ready

But persevere for in the end
there's so much more to know
to comprehend and assimilate
and countless shots to frame before
the truth can be exposed

A PERFECT DAY

It's a perfect day, with clear blue skies
no sign of rain, it feels worthwhile
to be alive
no past to mourn
no future dread
not seeking nor regretting
unproductive ventures
left behind

I bask in the euphoria
of this perfect feeling, before it's gone
and swept aside
by rising doubts
that I now attend
and fears from days long past
that in this point in time
do not belong

AND IT GROWS......

An affront and a slur directed my way
was it real or not? I cannot decide
but it hounds and torments my ramshackle brain
it refuses to die, and it grows
and it grows
and it grows
and it grows

And the more I resist, the greater its strength
till my anger's a monster, a titan, a brute
I swallow it whole to try and contain it
to quell and subdue, but it grows
and it grows
and it grows
and it grows

The beast is now mammoth, too big to repress
it erupts spitting venom, vomit and bile
and all who surround are defiled and polluted
yet for a short time, I feel better
then worse
then worse
then worse

And the after-effects can linger for years
as the injured all take a belief and a stake
the brute has now gone, but I'm left in a hole
to try and explain but I can't

But there's relative calm in the wake of the storm
as I grieve for my fall, at the feet of the wreck
but shortly thereafter, an affront, and a slur
and it starts up again, and it grows
and it grows
and it grows
and it grows

NO MORE

I've given up my quest to make you like me
I've lost my appetite for camouflage and masquerades
reciting words arranged and put in order
employing plots that I've explored
and a wealth of expertise
I've called upon
through books researched
and wisdom gained
but all along
I couldn't make the change I thought I would
therefore, I have withdrawn
resigned to solo, singular pursuits
and so, to new age thought and attitudes
and writings on the power of dreams, I say
no more
no more

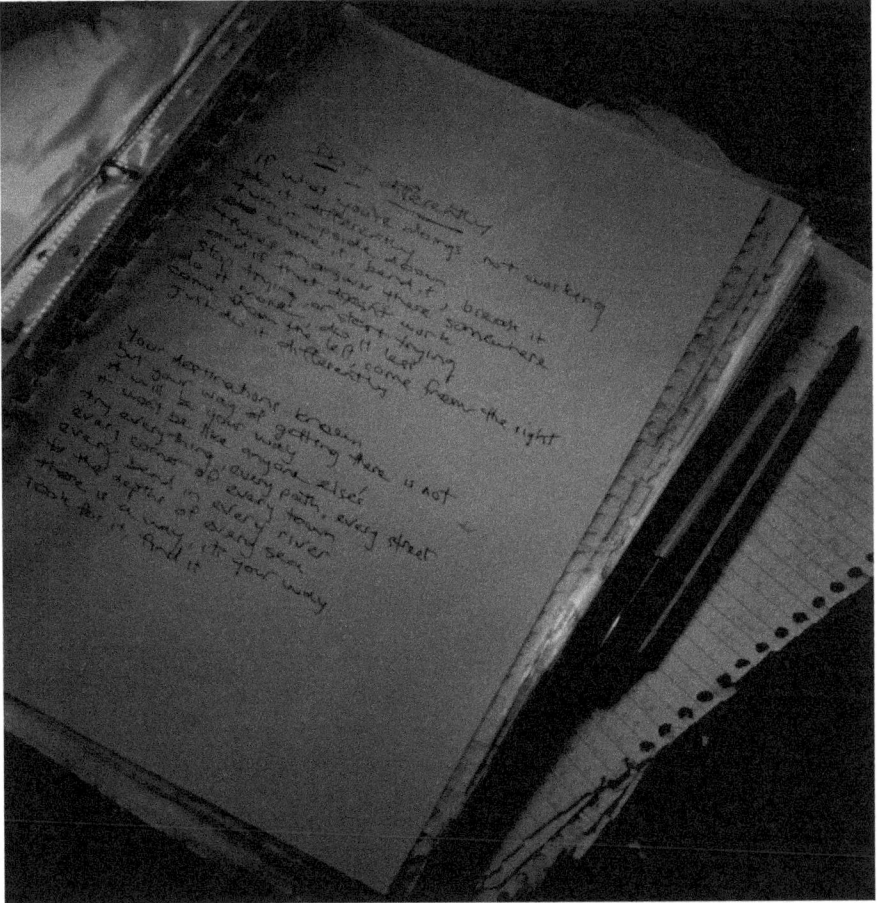

do it differently

if what you've always ... not working
if it isn't interesting
break it down, break it
turn it around, bend it / somewhere
moving ... if that answer there
So if that doesn't work
don't abandon ... start trying
... don't just do it ... come from the right
just do it differently

Your destinations known
... your way of getting there is not
it will be your way
it won't be like anyone else's
try everything, every path, every street
every corner of every town
to the banks of every river
there is a way of doing something
look for it. And do it your way

DO IT DIFFERENTLY

If what you're doing's not working
do it differently
turn it upside down
shake it
bend it
break it
there's an answer there somewhere
And if that doesn't work
stop trying
or start trying
do it more
do it less
come from the left
come from the right
just do it differently

Your destinations known
but your way of getting there is not
it will be your way
it won't be like anyone else's
Try everything
every path
every street
every corner of every town
every bend in every river
to the depths of every sea
there is a way
it's your way
look for it
find it

A TILLER OF THE SOIL

A tiller of the soil is what I am
no fanfare, not a hero nor a fake
like Abraham in Genesis, a servant through my toil
to feign a condescending pose would be an aberration
and from truth, a deviation
a lapse
a grave mistake.

With both hands on the plough, each field is done
we're judged upon the yield, the seed we sow
I work until the sun has gone beneath the far horizon
with one eye on the future, I prepare, I cultivate
the crops will soon be ready
I will tend them
row by row

A cog within a wheel I recognise
the role I play within the greater plan
my eyes are fixed upon my work, to God alone I kneel
to scrutinise, rehash or speculate upon my standing
may see me going backwards
to the place
where I began

On the task at hand, I focus and I dwell
what's good for you is good for me
and good for us as well

THE FUNERAL

Quietly we gathered, in our grief
"Abide with Me" played soft and gentle
we took our seats
and we pondered lives of discontent
and every vow not yet redeemed
and every chance that's come and gone
and hankerings abandoned
too severe
that never found their feet
to dance upon

I wonder did our late friend mourn the loss
of time not taken to explore
what lies beyond
what could have been, if he had sought
the truth, before he then forgot
his deepest lust, forbidden love
did he let it fall into
a shallow grave?
another funeral plot
to cry above

WHO AM I ?

On Monday I'd decided
upon a course
I confided in my friend
about my new direction forward
and he did endorse
my plan, my bold approach
but by Tuesday I had thrown those plans aside
increasingly unsure
of who I was

By Wednesday I'd been saved
I'd found the Lord
embracing my beliefs
I wore a cross around my neck
my life restored
and purged of sin and guilt
but by Thursday I'd become an atheist
still I was unsure
of who I was

Come Friday I felt blessed
I was in love
next day I knew the truth
it was a lie, another blow
to overcome
on Saturday I grieved
by Sunday I believed I was condemned
I hadn't yet discovered
who I was

SO SWEET

Cahoots
I think they are
I've been hoodwinked again
behind my back, they choose to plot
and cheat

First draft
don't judge too soon
and trust me when I say
I'll bend and graft until it is
complete

But no
they do not wait
and they assume the worst
and rush to swear an oath to my
defeat

No hope
beyond all doubt
a mind made up withdrawn
and tied up with a proper bow
so neat

But soon
I'll prove them wrong
and bruise their sorry creed
revenge will be a sip consumed
so sweet

I KEEP TO MYSELF THESE DAYS

I keep to myself these days, I am content
with my stories, my impressions of life
that I cannot forget
so I chronicle my thoughts and I try
to make some sense of what is left
after those reckless years
and after those mad and violent storms
I don't mourn their loss
I'm safer now
no longer stalking rank or new frontiers

I keep to myself these days, though half alive
satisfied with quiet pursuits
and a morning sky
and a muted breeze in the afternoon
but I remember when we arrived
side by side we'd march
arm in arm we'd fight
it was do or die back then
it's calmer now
the searing heat has cooled and long since passed

I keep to myself these days, my lesson learnt
I can no longer brave the risk and ruin
for so little return
the chaos and the confusion
it's a modest life that I now prefer
a safety-first routine
and travelling unattended
I try to spend my time
avoiding loss
protecting grace and pride and self-esteem

KEEPING UP

Am I keeping up with friends and folk
with money saved and left untouched?
I own so little, less than most
but they have lived hard-headed lives
while I've survived on angel dust

In business, they have found their place
with sober use of space and time
while I have gazed upon the stars
with sleepy eyes and errant whims
of epic tales and lullabies

They see a crack that should be filled
a gap in produce and supply
they build solutions fixed and proper
but they don't talk of Aristotle
or philosophies that question why

BOB DYLAN

He came from the upper mid-west, Minnesota
beset and drunk on the written word
he read Rimbaud
and "Bound for Glory"
and Jack Kerouac
and he sang the Dust Bowl ballads
but soon the lines dividing each
were blurred

He found his voice in the coffee houses
and village joints of Bleecker Street
a breeding ground
of primal thought
and ancient text
he married all in song
a collage of each impression
he would seek

But no maker's brand would he affix
to no masterplan would he submit
no censorship
designed to tether
would he observe
and no universal judgment
would see him bend his artistry
to fit

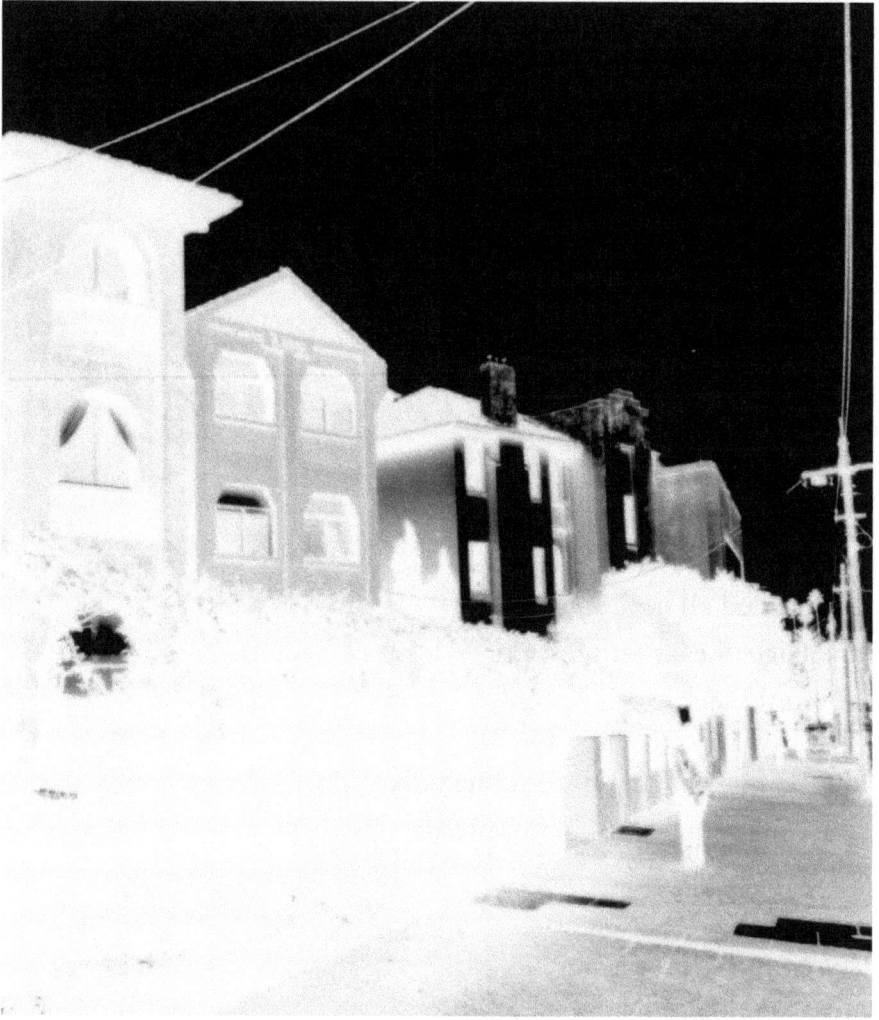

ANOTHER'S SHOES

Another's shoes and I may see it differently
I may reconsider a belief once set in stone
convictions may crumble
and leave me questioning
why I ever held that opinion in the first place
and why was I so adamant
about a fundamental I now disown

Another's shoes and I may join your noble cause
to change the assumptions of people once like me
before I experienced your pain
and felt your anguish
before I endured your grief and persecution
your dreams, your hopes, your prayers
before I saw the breach, the travesty

Another's shoes and I may cross-examine
every principle that I once held as true
every conclusion
and determination
that I once clung to so emphatically
may dissipate, dwindle, and die
when I taste first-hand the torment, that you've been through

INTO THE CHURCH I CREEP

Quietly into the church I creep
Ensemble voices sing "Abide with Me"
"What you sow you reap" the preacher warns the congregation
"And what is done is done" he says
and was always meant to be

I contemplate my life, my flawed existence
the pathway that I once resolved to tread
there's still a distance left, I am aware I have to travel
a stumbling block or two to overcome
still lay ahead

I wished to put some coins into the plate
though destitute am I, I can't pretend
and so, a simple message I create with pen and paper
a reflection on our world I've written down
and do extend

Not one above the rest, nor one below
and all will be a friend and not a foe

FAMOUS YEARS

It ended suddenly, we were not prepared
there was no bad blood, for we knew within
our famous years
had gone for good
our windfall spent
we said we're looking forward
to whatever the future brings

But each day since has been compared
to every sight we used to see
to every breath
we once took in
but falling short
so we feast on what remains
of all that used to be

PEOPLE LIKE US

People like us justify what we do
by reciting some words verbatim
that somebody threw us and so we believed
as they seemed a good fit with our personal style
our charisma, our wit, and our name

But for people like us, the truth is a lot
too rigid to even begin
we prefer a potboiler, an adage or two
easy to swallow and sweet in the mouth
the rest can be easily dismissed

And people like us find it hard on our own
we don't like to speak out of turn
while whispering low, so no one can hear
we speak of our truth and hope it will spread
I know, it's a little absurd

And we live in our bubbles and social routines
in our hands, our delusions are spun
and like broken machines we expect nothing more
than the daily procession of gossip and fault
it's a pity, for people like us

I CAN'T DECIDE

I'm afraid I can't decide
that worries me
I've tried to look ahead
at every possible result
if I proceed
one way or another
will I suffer if I'm wrong, should I wait
and complete the incomplete
I can't decide

So I make a judgment call
then think again
then I crawl into my shell
and reassess and scrutinize
what's in my head
a friend told me to act
it is a fact he claimed that nothing comes from nothing
is he right in what he said?
I can't decide

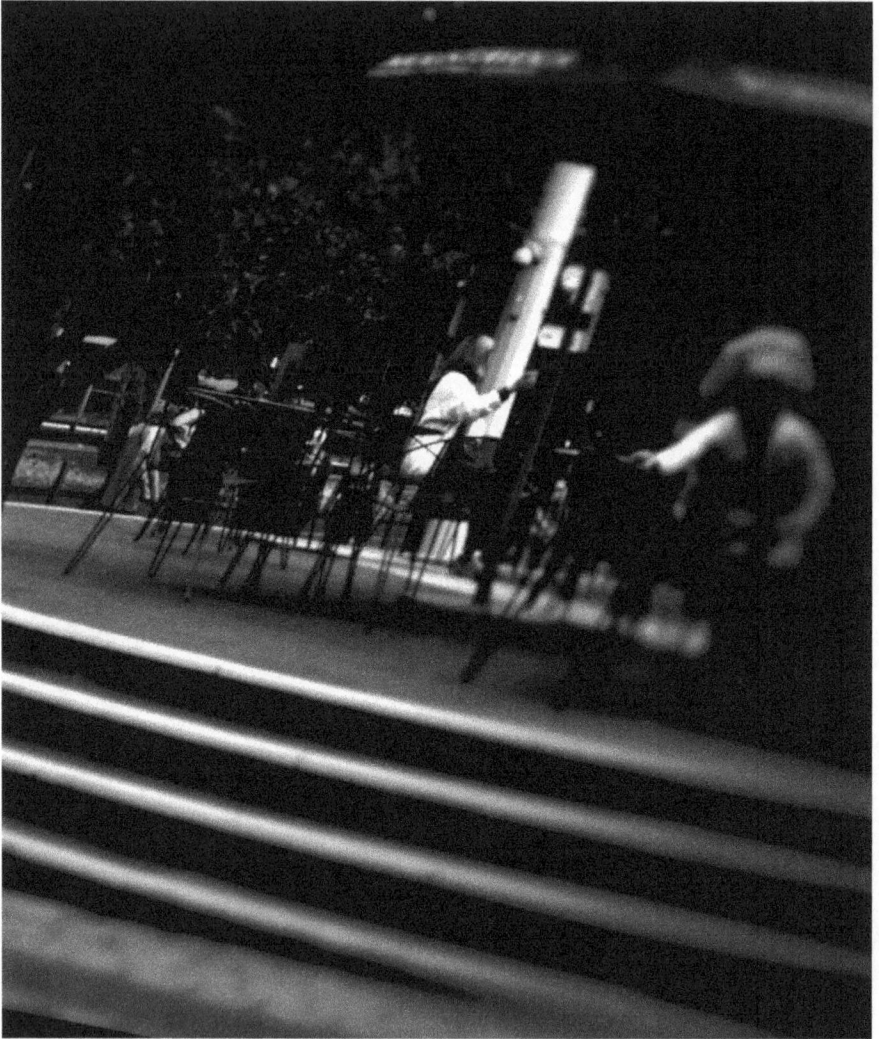

I'M STILL WAITING

I'm still waiting for you to say
you're sorry, it's the least I'm owed
until that day I'll tend my wound
though the bleeding stopped and ceased to be
a problem, years ago

And I'm still waiting for your approach
and simple acknowledgement
and to swear an oath to what you know
that I alone was the catalyst
on which you did depend

And I'm still waiting to make a start
for a sign that the way ahead
will not be marked by checks and crimps
and bitter pills rammed down my throat
that abstaining can prevent

And I'm still waiting to rid myself
of the emptiness within
and the hurt I've felt from a thoughtless deed
and the petulance that will not leave
and your words I can't forgive

I WILL

She whispered to me, give it one more try
you've come so far, why give up
persist, endure, survive
Crying out in anguish I confessed
I had no more to give, I'd done my best
and glad I'd surely be if I could rest a spell
and bid my constant thirst and want
a fond farewell
She said "You've not begun, you are not dead
do not accept the place you dwell
there's more to come
take up your sword
no point in giving up or standing still"
I shed a tear or maybe two
but to myself I said
I will… I will

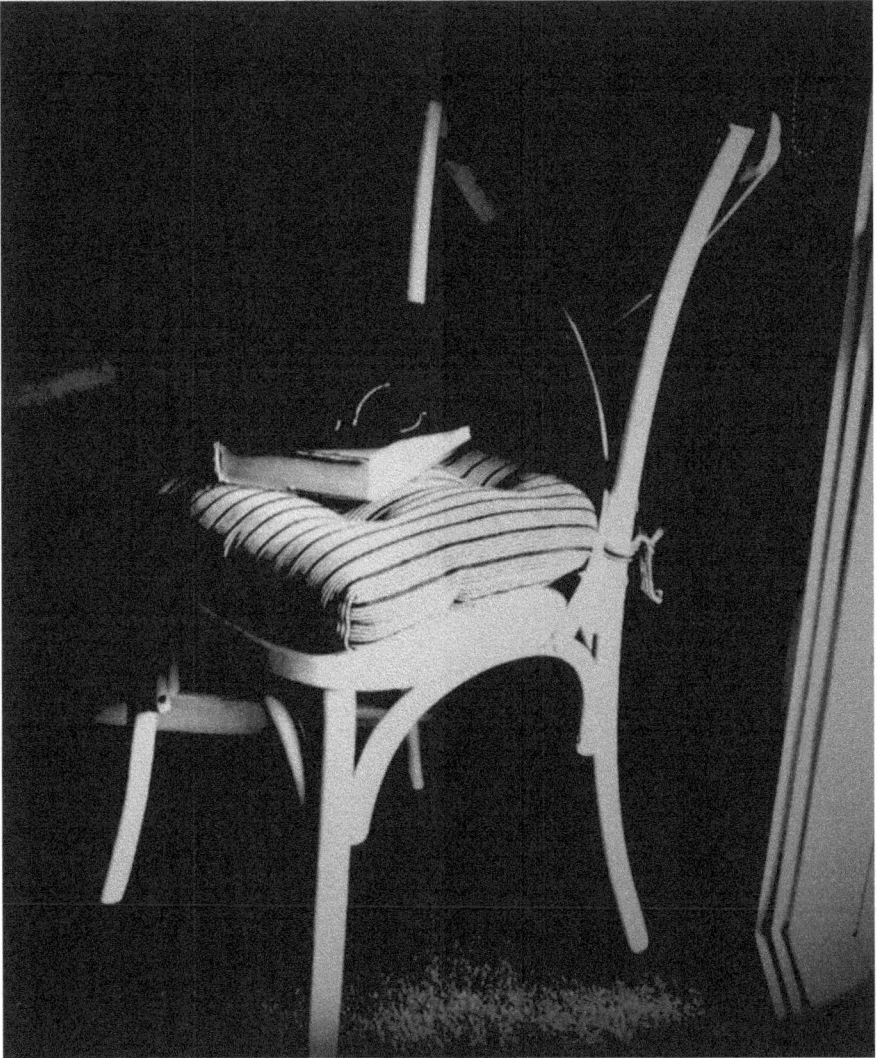

IF I WAS YOU

I'd know what to say and do, if I was you
the words would flow without restraint
my point of view
I'd clearly express and would explain
so not one soul could misconstrue
my meaning, then I'd take my shot
done with a perfect knack
and a faultless touch
that's if I was you
which clearly, I am not

I'd know how to think and feel, if I was you
doubt and dread would not prevail
I'd follow through
completing every deal that came
within my realm, within my field of view
I'd work and toil around the clock
and think divergent thoughts
and touch the moon
that's if I was you
which clearly, I am not

I know who I would be, if I was you
it's you I'd be and you alone
and that would do
it would be fine to always know
that all you touch, and hold as true
floats magically up to the top
no more fuss or friction
or discontent
that's if I was you
which clearly, I am not

GREEN

We are green
you are green, I am green
we stay green always
we think we're not but we are
we think we're making progress, but we're not
we think we're clever, but we're not
we think we make a difference, but we don't
we look down on others because they are green
even though we ourselves are green
history proves it
we drift aimlessly around the planet
engaging in pointless activities
while expounding concocted beliefs
someone else made up for us
it's pathetic
we worship the wrong gods
we honour the wrong deeds
we follow the wrong people
we think they have the answers
they don't
they are green
like us

THERE'S A PLACE

There's a place I'd like to visit
it's far away from here
I've chased its scent, its spell, its promise
my discontent a driving force
that's made me persevere

It is access that I'm seeking
so I can dance at last
to grasp my share of gain and splendour
it's in the air, just out of reach
the door is still ajar

I've seen a grand ideal
that I could recreate
so I persist with my endeavours
my workmanship I bend to please
that maybe my mistake

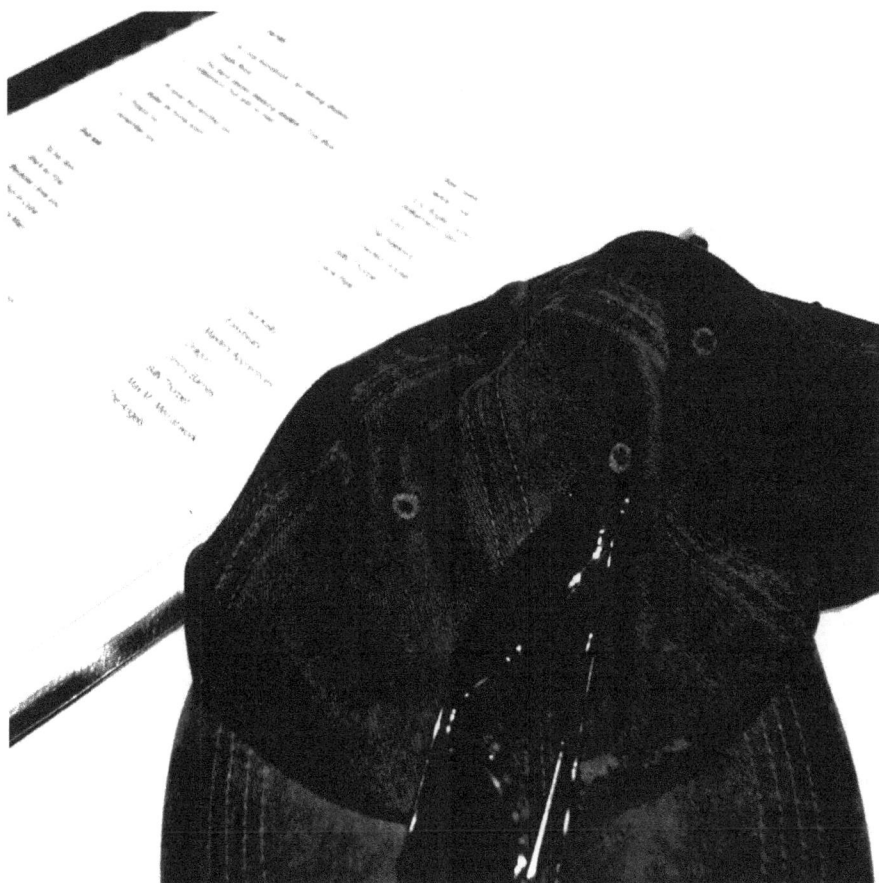

LUNATIC ASYLUM

In this lunatic asylum
we take all we can get
we covet stuff and trinkets
and every item purchased
nullifies our pain and suffering
and averts our discontent

In this weird and desperate madhouse
escape is our crusade
from room fifteen to eighty-one
we knock on every doorway
but every room we enter
is different yet the same

In this flaky, flipped-out snake pit
we love our idle chatter
we spit out worthless drivel
with neighbours, friends, and cohorts
on a range of different subjects
but none that really matter

In this vulgar institution
we ravage, starve, and kill
and when we're not, we gather
riches from the ruins
we do it for the power
for the Lord, and for the thrill

In this deviant foundation
we like to entertain
with a charity fundraiser
we cry fictitious tears
for the needy and the hungry
when we know that from ourselves
our minds do rarely stray

A FORMULA

I stumbled on a formula
that completely changed my life
achieved by governing my state of mind
remaining free of any thought
while performing named endeavour
took me from underdog to samurai

I kept a watch upon my brain
to guarantee it stayed
unoccupied to keep all channels open
allowing intuition free
unhindered by myself
I went from scarcity to overflowing

Was this really me I thought
for I seemed uninvolved
as if a greater force were in my place
it wasn't me I did conclude
for I'd removed myself
and let the heavens oversee my fate

A FORTUNATE DAY

It was a fortunate day, now that I look back
although it was painful, at the time
a surprising end
abrupt and barbed
a stark cliché
the risk I'd never take
if left to my control
and enterprise

The catalyst, I'm in your debt
a flame was lit, as if by chance
the grand reveal
when forced to brave
dismay and fear
a better path emerged
where I never dared imagine
I'd advance

IF I'M NOT CAREFUL

I could be homeless and dispossessed
if I'm not wise and circumspect
out on the streets
a rootless man
if indiscreet
I should fortify my house
with weapons of intent

I could be jilted and down in the dumps
and cast aside to bear the brunt
of being left
disconsolate
I should protect
myself by taking charge
of your head, and your hands, and your heart

I could be broke and penniless
destitute, at the bitter end
if I'm not sane
my money could
evaporate
I should bury it in a hole
before it's all been spent

I could die from some disease
in pain and woe and disappear
from the face of the earth
if only life
could be preserved
I should have my body frozen
cryogenically

And a laughingstock, I may well be
a fool, a clown, if I reveal
my inner thoughts
my hopes, my dreams
they should be ignored
and safely locked away
where they can bring no shame to me

I LOOKED DOWN FROM MY WINDOW

I looked down from my window
at the wretched streets below
I saw the desperate starving millions
as they banged upon my door
I heard their pleas turn from a murmur
to a burgeoning crescendo
a deafening explosion
a monumental roar

I looked down from my window
at a scene I've come to know
I saw the exiles and the outlaws
and the ones who disappear
I saw the homeless and the injured
the ravenous, the starving
the elderly forgotten
the despair of volunteers

I looked down from my window
to a place I dare not go
I saw the war-torn buildings crumble
as they fell into the sea
I saw one man dictate to others
who would live and who would die?
who could enter, who could marry?
who'd be bound and who'd be free

I looked down from my window
where the windstorms howl and blow
I saw an old man seeking shelter
from the bleak and bitter cold
and though he built this lucky country
with his sweat and with his toil
there's no money in the budget
for the sick or for the old

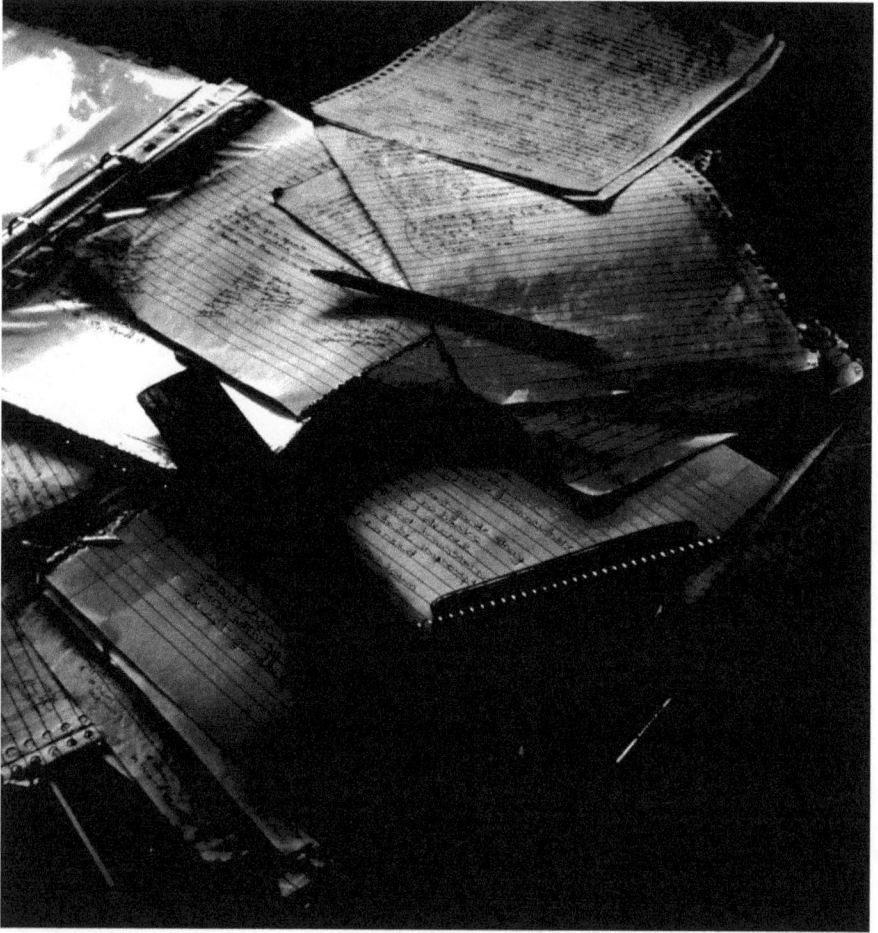

INSIDE MY HEAD

I become entrenched inside my head
where my loyal friend and I meet every day
and we talk of Kant and Socrates
of Hemingway, Voltaire and William Bligh
and I please myself, I'm no man's pawn
and no holding company's slave

In my fabricated universe
I do immerse myself in rude ambition
and my sturdy friend will play the part
if she's Selena, I'll be Valentine
and we disregard their condemnation
their vulgar opposition

Each day I stay a little longer
a fast and wanton lust for bliss
tied up in my imagination
a trickle, minuscule, becomes a flood
I'm stranded but I cling to life
to ensure I do not sink

PATTI SMITH

Each work of art
she pulls apart
the gospel from the myth
deceit beware
there'll be no care
from the pen of Patti Smith

Impassioned verse
a defiant curse
and a frenzied monologue
an abrasive plea
from Patti Lee
has the bite of a prairie dog

Salvation found
in pages bound
and words that wake the dead
with God they spar
like a wrecking bar
as they clear the way ahead

A rebellious fist
is raised and kissed
you can hear the old ground shake
and you can't go back
and join the pack
once you've walked in Patti's wake

INTERVIEW

We can't offer you the position unfortunately
You're not the type of person we're looking for

We are after someone more qualified
But not too qualified
Articulate
But not outspoken
With a sense of humour
Though not outrageous
Serious
But not too serious
Honest
Obviously
Young
But not too young
Experienced
But not too old
White
Yes (but we are an equal opportunity employer)
Male
Preferably (but we are an equal opportunity employer)
Punctual
Always

You don't qualify
Goodbye

THANK YOU

Thank you for the gift
it arrived on time
if I made a list of all
the lucky breaks that I've received
I'd write and write
without an end in view
and to the moon and back it would extend
to my blessings I am wise
and overwhelmed

And thank you for the word
it filtered through
I was concerned but now
I understand acknowledgement
and gratitude
are all I'll ever need
to guarantee that riches propagate
like interest that's accrued
and multiplies

MORNING, NOON AND NIGHT

The morning's air is fresh with hope
when dreamers dare to fantasize
the quiet streets
awakened bones
the brand-new light
for those who view the world
through zealous eyes

But afternoons can take their toll
as unease looms and starts to grow
the stale routine
as another day
is slipping by
the feeling of malaise
I've come to know

Nightfall marks a change in mood
embracing darkness fills the hole
the void disguised
by T V snacks
and movie madness
but soon it's dawn again.............

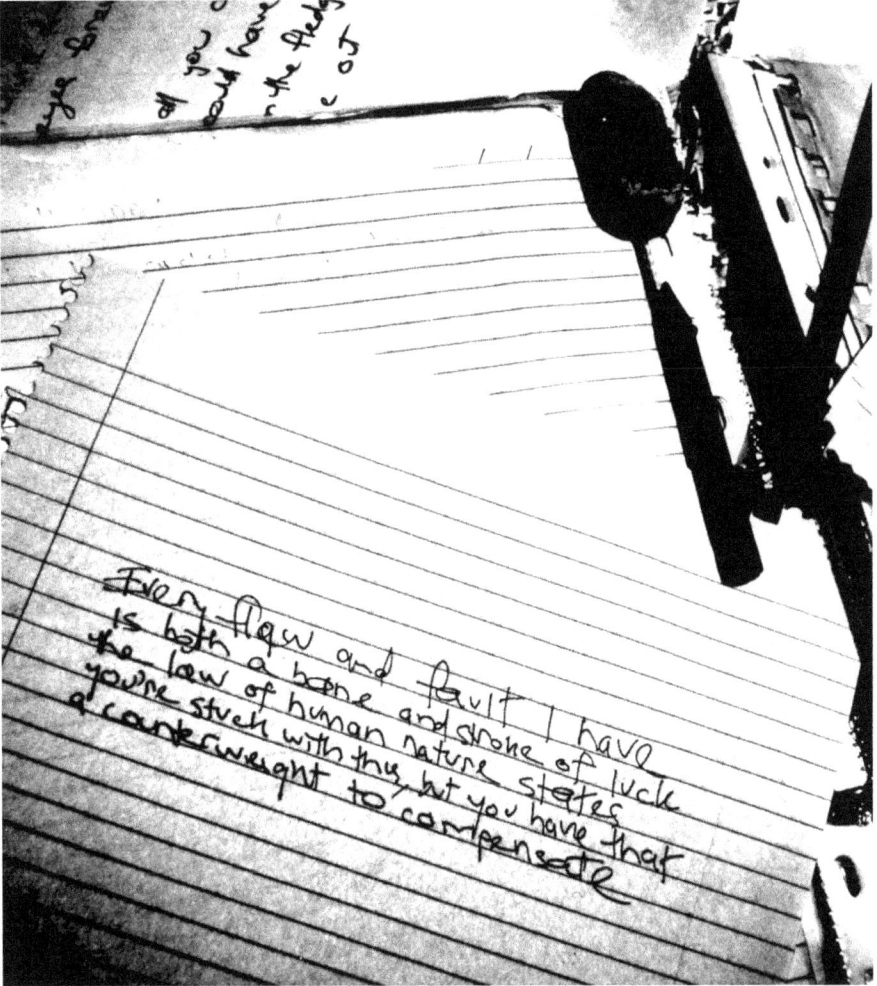

Every flaw and fault I have
is both a bane and stroke of luck
the law of human nature states
you're stuck with this, but you have that
a conterweight to compensate

LET'S KEEP IT SUPERFICIAL

Let's keep it superficial, artificial, commonplace
so no one is offended, ill at ease
civility protected, let us do what is proposed
endeavouring to charm and not demean nor aggravate
but please with faultless manners, as we go
so no one is resentful or alarmed

A fire burns within, but let's put on a stupid grin
and talk about the weather all day long
and let's not speak with candour, that's unwanted, so unkind
let's keep the truth at bay, what we want's a genteel pose
for grace and protocol is not a crime
so let's pretend, it's easier that way

But what if we were bolder and we spoke of love and fear
and how we came to be the way we are
and secrets were unveiled, not distorted, or concealed
then we could cease this futile and bizarre timidity
I'm sure it wouldn't be a large ordeal
if we were purposeful and resolute

LIKE DISAPPEARING INK

Like disappearing ink
it's gone
it was here yesterday
but now it's vanished off the face of the earth
"did you move it?"
"you did didn't you?"
I desperately need it
if I can't find it
I'm not sure what I'll do
I'll have to give up completely or start again
that's how important it is
It's frustrating, I can't believe this is happening to me
oh, hold on……..
……..I've found it…….

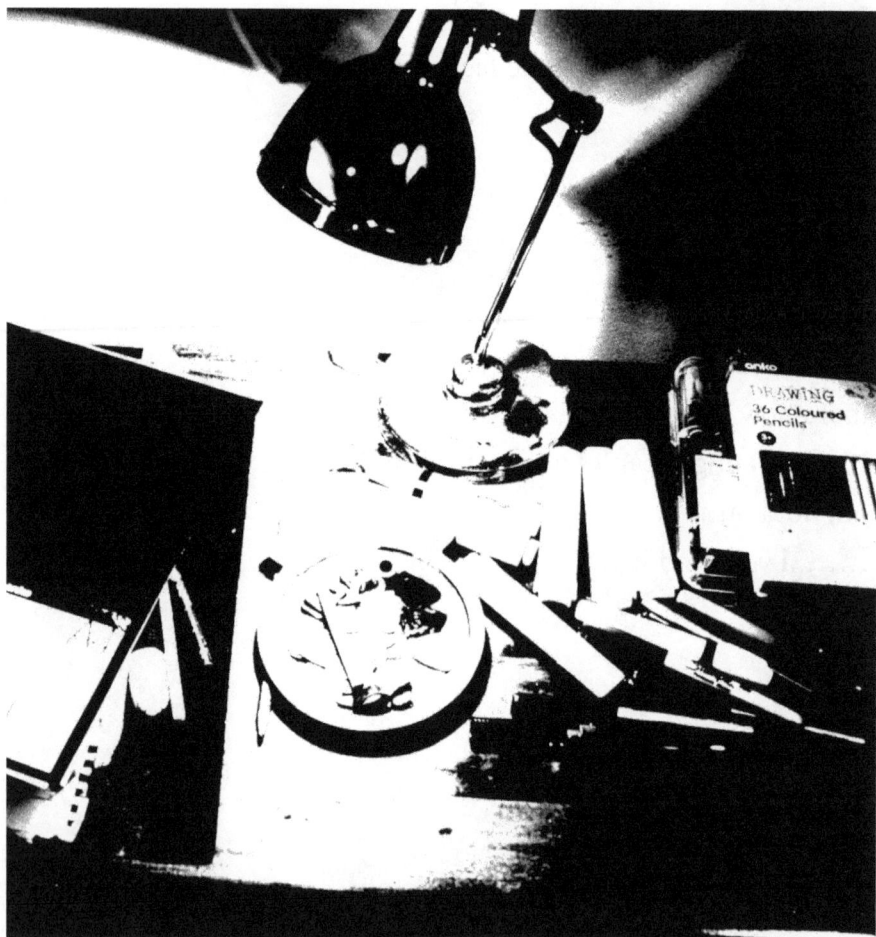

A SINGLE VOICE

A single voice can still be heard
above the noise, the grating din
it tells the truth
composed, at ease
not raised in anger
but not afraid to face
a tyrant or a king

A single voice can stir a nation
and reach the corners of the earth
and old beliefs
are swept aside
and all at once
a new direction forward
is formed and given birth

A single cry can raise a country
that's paralysed by fear and doubt
and the disadvantaged
and oppressed
are given voice
and those estranged are nourished
where once they'd go without

A single word can make a difference
a declaration, strong and tough
an emphatic no
is said with purpose
a line is drawn
it states with firm intention
......enough is enough

THEY ASKED ME IF I LIKED YOU

They asked me if I liked you
no, I had to say
you were tall and self-absorbed
your voice, a touch abrasive
bristling with conceit
your attire was not to my taste

And you had a careless gait
as if you didn't care
for others speculation
they said you were persuasive
in your style and presentation
a view I didn't share

To me, you were an actor
a scam I did conclude
I told my friend my knowledge
my theories calculative
he said "Maybe the problem
is that he, is not like you"

THIS SONG

I sang this song in my tender years
locked in my room, remote and apart
a winter's lament, a tender motif
it fell from the heavens, it fell from the stars
And through every loss, despair, and heartbreak
I sang it with spirit, it carried the load
though partners I had, are now done and departed
that song is still with me, from so long ago
So I gave up my heart, my future as well
to follow the romance, the verse and the rhyme
when you left I kept singing it, over and over
to heal what was broken and to keep what was mine
But I know if I met you, now everything's gone
we'd remember the laughter, the joy, and the song

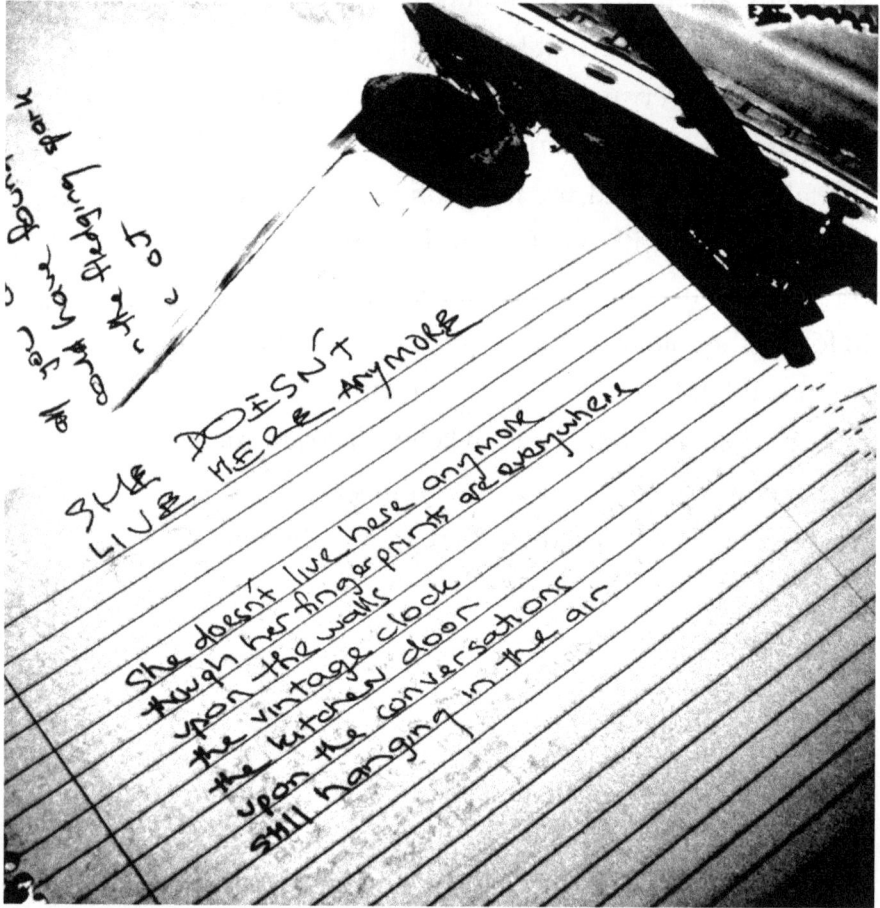

SHE DOESN'T
LIVE HERE ANYMORE

She doesn't live here anymore
though her fingerprints are everywhere
upon the walls
the vintage clock
the kitchen door
upon the conversations
still hanging in the air

90

DEAR ACQUAINTANCE

Dear Acquaintance

Thank you for the conversation today
it was great to catch up with you again
and thanks for telling me
all that's happened in your life
I hope I looked suitably interested
even though I wasn't.
You obviously don't consider
any detail about yourself
too insignificant to leave out.
I hope I nodded and smiled
at the appropriate times.
And thanks for not asking
a single thing about me.
Anything that reduced our time together
was gratefully received.
Hopefully, I won't run into you
again anytime soon.

Regards

NEVER

I've never been to Paris or New York
I've never found my way to Cameroon
or Bangalore
and the door may now be closing
on my plans to be the best
I'll have to be appeased with commonplace
or something less

I've never healed the rift 'tween you and me
I've never found the motive or a reason
to proceed
and the meaning of my life
I cannot grasp or comprehend
and the plans we made have faded, I often wonder
where they went

No riches have I made in stocks and bonds
no land of milk and honey have I found
or chanced upon
and the book I longed to write
is still a notion, nothing more
and what used to be a craving is now indifference
an afterthought

A fruitless life it seems I have endured
but I met a man who told me I have nothing
left to prove
what he assumed surprised me
was he wrong or was he right?
it occurred to me we judge ourselves with a pitiless
critic's eye

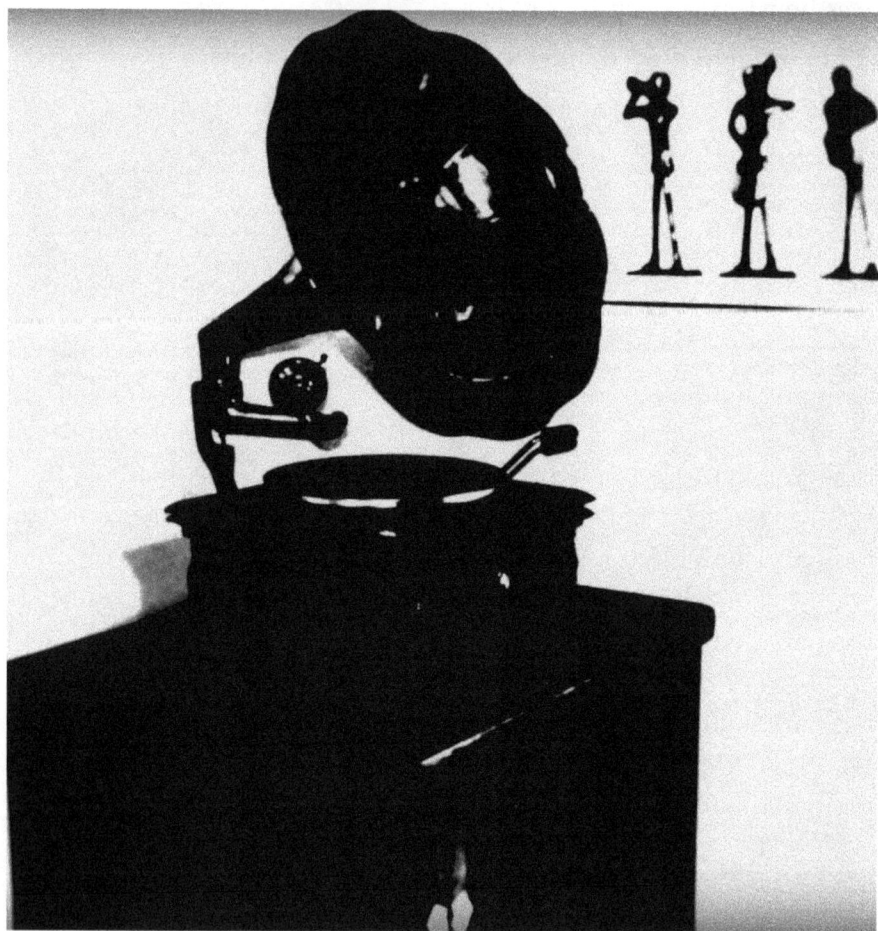

A STEP

A step is just a step
but not a step if you can see below
so far to fall, so critical
I know it must be done
eventually, regrettably

It's now become a leap
a mammoth feat, this one straightforward step
It's grown a spike and devil's horns
I mourn the loss of simple pleasures
now driven from my head

And yet I can't begin
what I once did with ease, instinctively
before it loomed with earnest weight
to bleed away my pluck and nerve
betrayed by thoughts, stiff-necked and foul
that hunt and shadow me

At last, I took the step
yet incorrect to say that fate was kind
I stumbled, fell, and looked a clown
yet courage gained I stepped again
and found at last that I could say
"This time I think I'm fine"

AN ACCIDENT

It wasn't meant to happen, but it did
an unforeseen calamity
a slip, an oversight
that didn't fall within my strategy, the plans I'd made
I'd have to readjust and learn the value of discretion
and learn to trust myself again
and to live with my mistake

I rushed ahead completely unprepared
and feeling game and bulletproof
I dared to speculate
"When will you learn to think again," they said "You're not
equipped"
I should have sought a wiser head to counsel and instruct
and recognize some things cannot be forced
or made to fit

But in the aftermath of all that was explored
I wonder, did I play a part
or more, a leading role
attracting each occurrence, though remaining unaware
the science of the mind can be a dark magnetic force
its power great as any act
or words composed in prayer

SCATTERED

Once we were united by our fervour and our quest
a purpose more important than ourselves
a common bond established; every interference banned
our focus was defined and parallel, sympatico
not overwhelmed, but purposeful and fixed
and those who weren't on board were left behind

To bring about a change was our desire, our call to arms
we'd march into the streets to make it clear
our movement would emancipate what once seemed ironclad
and those who'd been betrayed and lived in fear would find accord
and tears of joy would spill on the bloodied ground
and the hardest rock would crumble, come the day

But soon our holy war became outdated and banal
the songs that we embraced, now a cabaret
our lofty aspirations never did eventuate
and one by one we turned to other games to fill our time
the chains of fellowship we did create
now scattered to every corner of the earth

IT'S PROBABLY ME

I like to creep around the edges, the outskirts
the fringes of society
always looking in, observing
and watching from a distance
it suits me
I've embraced who I am
I'm an onlooker
an eye- witness
quietly documenting the madness of the human race
and my own madness
in fact, I don't know who's more deranged
you or me
it's probably me

RECONCILE

A   I'd like to reconcile and start again
for if not now my flesh and blood
when will the time be right?
when will we see an end to this impasse?
please do convey
will it be this year or maybe next
or not at all?
your thoughts upon this point I'd like to hear
without delay

        B   You never loved me

A   I'm here to talk, but will not take the blame
for something you've concocted
that is baseless, childish nonsense
why don't you put aside the pointless rancour
you extol
and carry round your neck, like you aspire
to be a victim
your statements I reject, your discontent
is not my fault

        B   You never loved me
              You never loved me
              You never loved me

              You still can't say it, can you?

100

THE SPECTATOR

We watch and judge, assess and rate
we then discuss, how they performed
and what we'd do
if we were them
which we are not
upon their fixed endeavours
our fortune's rise and fall

But what of us, in this design
reduced to dust, we wilt and fade
a follower
a passive drone
a limp bystander
not building nor inventing
not yearning to create

No viewing chair, though soft and warm
can be compared, to being immersed
inside the fray
where danger looms
with every breath
where lions seek their prey
and will not be deterred

THE TRUTH

Tell me no lies, no vague untruth, no cunning storyline
no fabricated subterfuge, no bogus trickery
don't make believe or try to weave an artificial brief
the truth persists and will prevail
it has no axe to grind
no tale to chronicle
no favours to redeem

Don't change the facts, they can't mutate to save your reputation
they can't be moved from here to there, to aid your troubled state
don't speculate or ruminate, the truth is set in stone
it won't adjust to minimize
your anguish or your plight
your lapses, your regrets
your crisis or your shame

It cannot be improved upon, destroyed, or reconditioned
it's ready to reveal itself, it never goes away
it lies in wait, but knows its fate, on the bottom of the sea
but bit by bit, it makes its move
and rises to the surface
and resumes its rightful place
in the buoyant light of day

AN EXPLANATION

If I could give you an explanation
a blow-by-blow communique
I'd tell you how it all unfolded
each bump and block I've had to face

But I have stumbled back and forward
without a guide or secret map
so now the truth I wish to tell you
there never was a master plan

No strategy that you could follow
just blunders, slips and oversights
that somehow worked to my advantage
I can't explain the reason why

A plot is fine but will succumb
to unplanned blessings and random luck

THIS YEAR

This year I will be bolder, less afraid
I'll bear each blow that's served and still advance
to risk potential loss will be my purpose
and fear will be shot down at my command
This year I will not waste another moment
trying to be someone else but me
keeping my identity unpublished
will not be what I do, this coming year
This year I will remember to acknowledge
every stroke of luck that's come my way
and I'll attract the favour of creation
and the universe will foster my crusade
And though I may be shunned and cast adrift
from where I come ashore, I will begin

FRIENDS

I don't expect we'll ever be friends again
that won't happen
it was bound to end badly
and it did
I blame you
you blame me
the usual story

But I've moved on
I'm guessing you have too
but I can't pretend to be blind to what I've seen
or unaware of what I've done
since you …..
which makes it impossible to go back

These days I'm leaving room for me
you took up so much space
but it was good for a while
and I'm grateful for that

THINK

Listen
stop mouthing words
flimsy and vaporous
sweepings, that have no ambition
no weight

Ponder
for a moment
something beyond yourself
beyond your drivelling, humdrum
routine

The stars
the universe
the code of the mystics
have you ever contemplated
these things

Never
would be my guess
your endless narration
of every detail of your life
confounds

So think
before you speak
of trite, mundane concerns
there's more than common, simple fare
to taste

www.ingramcontent.com/pod-product-compliance
Lightning Source LLC
LaVergne TN
LVHW041159080426
835511LV00006B/664